COOKIES FOR A ROYAL SNACK

Lalie Harcourt &
Ricki Wortzman

Illustrated by Vesna Krstanovic

Dominie Press, Inc.

Annie is the royal baker.
She loves baking cookies.

The royal family loves
the cookies Annie bakes.
She never makes
the same cookie twice.

The prince likes cookies for his morning snack.

Annie thinks about the prince.
She moves the shapes
and makes a ...

... kite.

"Oh," says the prince,
"that kite looks
good enough to eat."
And he ate it!

The queen likes cookies for her afternoon snack.

Annie thinks about the queen.
She moves the shapes
and makes a ...

... flower.

"Oh," says the queen,
"that flower looks
good enough to eat."
And she ate it!

The king likes cookies for his bedtime snack.

Annie thinks about the king.
She moves the shapes
and makes a ...

... crown.

"Oh," says the king,
"that crown looks
good enough to eat!"
And he ate it!

Annie likes cookies, too.